Praise for *The Art of Job Hunting*

Anastasia Helena Fenald's work is an endless ride down every emotional avenue workers must pass to find a job. A sincere and at times humorous juxtaposition between looking for work and self-reflection, but most importantly, a touch of cultural richness to the working class that is often unseen and unappreciated. This is one of the best collections out there. It is truly unique.

> —Ceasar K. Avelar, Poet Laureate of Pomona, California & Author of *God of the Air Hose and Other Blue-Collar Poems*

A funny, albeit painfully true, parody of the experience of job hunting in the age of late-stage capitalism. I cackled out loud, shook my fist at The Man, and renewed my allegiance to the working-class hero. I even shed tears as I read the manuscript in preparation for publication in between scouting job listings on Indeed and Idealist. This poetic dramedy is a lyrical lifeline for anyone drowning in the throes of job hunting. As the poet reminds us, we are more than this!

> —Brenda Vaca, Author of *Riot of Roses* & Founder of Riot of Roses Publishing House

In her second poetry collection, *The Art of Job Hunting*, Anastasia Helena Fenald presents an intelligently hilarious portrayal of the horrors often associated with job seeking.

Using her witty persona and her mastery of language, Fenald sets the reader up on a job interview from hell and modifies the strenuous world of the job seeker into an artistic endeavor by painting a bold, humoristic alternative to the conventionally harsh realities of inequality within America's job industry.

> —Carlos Ornelas, Author of *Ketchup: Sopa de Gato* & the forthcoming *Villain's Vernacular*

The Art of Job Hunting catapults us through the acrobatic cartwheels of trying to land the "dream" job. This riveting poetry collection navigates the torturous truths of today's job seeking maze, highlighting all the hoops we must jump through just to survive. From rejection letters to toxic bosses, Anastasia Fenald weaves in potent satire with honest revelations that challenge how to pursue the "American dream" and still keep our dignity.

—Alex Petunia, Author of *Tending My Wild*

Anastasia Fenald's new collection is poignant and biting in its witty critique of the dreadful nature of job searching for the everyday working class, whose labor is often unappreciated or exploited. The poems highlight the formalic way the capitalist system diminishes workers' humanity into replaceable parts of a machine. It acknowledges the struggles of average people while scoffing sarcastically at the employment contract of servitude we sign for survival.

—James Coats, Author of *Midnight and Mad Dreams*

The Art of Job Hunting

THE ART OF JOB HUNTING

Dramedy in Verse

ANASTASIA HELENA FENALD

RIOT OF ROSES
PUBLISHING HOUSE
SEJATNGA
UNCEDED TONGVA TERRITORY
SOUTH WHITTIER, CALIFORNIA

Published by Riot of Roses Publishing House

The Art of Job Hunting
Copyright © 2023, Anastasia Helena Fenald
ISBN: 978-1-961717-02-2 (paperback)
ISBN: 978-1-961717-09-1 (hardback)
ISBN: 978-1-961717-03-9 (ebook)
ISBN: 978-1-961717-04-6 (audio)
Library of Congress Control Number: 2023947430

First Edition, 2023

Printed in the United States of America.

www.riotofrosespublishinghouse.com

Cover design by Anastasia Helena Fenald & Emily Anne Evans
Layout design by Emily Anne Evans
Edited by Elle B. Parker
Editor-in-Chief, Brenda Vaca

this book is for recent college grads

this book is for working moms & dads

this book is for minimum wage workers

this book is for unemployed veterans

this book is for every disabled person

this book is for all kinds of women

this book is for voices in a second language

this book is for washed up artists

this book is for broke ass people

this book is for disenfranchised dreamers

this book is for forgotten capitalist cogs

this book is for every broken promise

this book is for righteous anger

this book is for bitter people

this book is for job seekers

this book is for you

&

this book is absolutely for me

Contents

Preface

This is not a job help book. This is a burn capitalism to the ground book. This is my bitter revenge for applying to over 300 jobs after finishing my M.A. in 2016. I only got hired for a part-time position at the local car dealership to make $10.50 an hour.

See, when I was born in 1992, the U.S. unemployment rate might have been 7.4% and the federal minimum wage was $4.25, but an average gallon of gas cost $1.13.

Last year, in 2022, our unemployment rate was 3.4%, federal minimum wage $7.25, but an average gallon of gas cost $4.90.

So, in 1992, with the federal minimum wage of $4.25 per hour, we only would have paid 27% of that hour per one gallon of gas versus paying 67% of the working hour in 2022 for our one-gallon gas.

And yes, it could be considered a little funny about how in 1992 apparently the best city to live in was in Sioux Falls, South Dakota versus living in the bustling City of Atlanta, Georgia in 2022, but even 30 years ago, the economy was stronger with the annual GDP Growth being at 3.5% in 1992 versus the only 2.1% in 2022.

We continue to operate in a deficit. Everything is more expensive now, and it requires that we do so much more to achieve a similar prosperity. Year after year, companies have recorded record profits, but the dollars in our pockets are worth less now. We are only left with:

- Higher Inflation:
  7% (2022) vs. 2.9% (1992)

- Rise in the average cost of U.S. homes:
  $449,300 (2022) vs. $121,500 (1992)

- More education for growing industries:
  Nurse Practitioner (2022) vs. Service Industry (1992)

It shouldn't be a surprise then, like you, I'm angry. I'm annoyed. I'm tired of doing everything that worked for my parents and grandparents told me to do, only to watch it fail me attempt after attempt. This book is my own manifesto expressing the truths we are not allowed to voice in those job applications, assessments, and interviews. Think of it as a truth serum and don't worry about the consequences. Why cry and write political essays when you can laugh in some poem parodies?

The Art of Job Hunting

Give Me That Career Chip

job hunting is akin to crochett
a sister to layered cake
      a time-loop   disguised as a hell loop
applications
      assessments   interviews
knot   &   twist
     in   e n d l e s s i n f i n i t y
         beginnings   &   endings
               alpha   &   omega
tangled
little yarn balls
some   shapeless unknown
          monetary   promise

and I wonder/ if my fingers are nimble needles/ to shred the threads/ of all my expectations/ pluck the definition of my value/ when I start over/ and over/ when I end over/ and over/ waiting for a single acceptance in a sea of rejections/ waiting for the gospel good news/ waiting like Seymour on the sidewalk from that one Emmy Award Winning episode of Futurama/ waiting and waiting and waiting/ until I am only left bitter and angry/ fire & rage/ but still begging/ while I fantasize about all the ways I'll destroy the one percent/ plot out my revenge/ where my hunt becomes a haunt as I actually poltergeist myself in some rich man's pocket/ and we fall in love/ hand in hand/ sweet creatures to be married/ stand beside him as he grows weak on the stairwell after our honeymoon/ watch him fall/ scream his name telenovela slow motion/ my fingers brush his arm as he tumbles/ my attempt to save him/ throw myself over his body when the paramedics come/ sob at his funeral into an embroidered handkerchief with his initials/ wear a black veil with evening gown gloves/ search my purse for red lipstick next to his will and some unmarked gum with too much caffeine/ dab my tears/ take a deep breath of Versace/ scan the reception/ and bullseye my way into a new man's pocket whose heart is less than sturdy too.

Ok Google, Define Job

job *noun*
1. a paid position of regular employment.
2. a task or piece of work, especially one that is paid.
3. a way to give oneself value, to determine
         if one is worthy, a hope that by
         performing this action,
         they can be fed,
                        housed,
                                respected.
         jobs are breath,
life memories,
                        legacies   passed
         down in stories
         heralding one's
                  obedience,
compliance, ability to never
                                ask for more
                                when one is already
         so *lucky*
                        to be employed & not forgotten.
to be full & not hungry.

         to be useful & not rusted.

         don't you know work is how the poor die?
         why do you think the rich search for eternal life?

The Art of Job Hunting

Sometimes, I treat my résumé like a work of art. I align all the bullet points in symmetric minimalism; sculpt the working content with chiseled precision; pad my experience with bold saturation. Write that I "single-handedly managed the successful upgrade & deployment of new environmental illumination." Call it my bright lights installation, call it my sly silver tongue disguising the orchestration of changing a lightbulb's replacement. In other words, I know how to turn the lights back on. In other words, I know how to do the dirty work.

Sometimes, I borrow my first impressions from Monet. Water-colored beauties that melt with nervous sweat at networking events, tucked away in hotel ballrooms like a Fibonacci sequence. I smudge the edges of my suit I've had since high school, a muddy mousy brown original. A Dalí interruption amongst the clean lines of mass-produced white cardstock; against the sharp lines of MBAs and trust-fund babies and fraternity brotherhoods; against the sweet curves of beautiful interns serving cocktails on their plattered degrees; against the suffocating, prestigious, corporate elite.

Sometimes, in the glory of the job hunt, I say "sphinx me a riddle" as I pop art against Andy Warhol, slide into an interview line as if getting a mugshot and I smile secret like the Mona Lisa, as my heartbeat flutters in confusion, dances like Degas' ballerinas in excitement while I juggle dodgeball questions such as:

"Where do you see yourself in five years?"
"What is your biggest weakness?"
"If you could take one thing to a desert island, what would it be?"

Sometimes, in all that is my bravado, I falter in the interview. I color outside the lines. I am unable to paint myself as someone beautiful. My ambition eats me like acid rain, erases all that I have molded from clay, erodes me into grit that can't make anything. I am reminded that job hunting is not for the weak, not for the meek, not for timid little children dressed in college robes because we are only prey of the capitalist machine. We are only deer stalked with disappointment shot through our futures. We are only naïve little things to think our art will start a revolution. We are only preschool chalk masquerading as oil paint.

Sometimes, if not always, our value depreciates with our every breath not spent being hung in museums like all the van Goghs, the Kahlos, the Picassos, and our usefulness deteriorates and our résumés mold like unsold art found at the swap meets. We are asked in every application, in every interview why there is a gap in our employment, like those years we stood in the unemployment line was akin to a five-star vacation on the white sandy beaches of the Cayman Islands, like we could afford to have accounts connected to the Cayman Islands.

Sometimes, but maybe all the time, there is guilt when using our EBT card to buy the simple things: milk, eggs, and cheese, but the world acts as if we only eat fine filet mignon feasts, as if we do not forage for any opportunity, as if we do not get swindled trying to sell Cutco knives, Mary Kay, and Amway; as if the word "no" holds the entirety of our vocabulary and we decline employment because we're waiting for the next BEST thing; as if we can afford to wait for the next best thing; as if our integrity in society is only worth questioning when we produce nothing —
as if our unemployment means
we are nothing.

There is an art to job hunting and **sometimes** I wish I was fluent in the same way the brushstrokes stain the canvas.

I wish I didn't need to be hired on my own merit. I wish I could pretend all the demeaning jobs I worked before were not so demeaning and maybe for once, someone gives me a <u>fucking</u> handout, someone plucks me off the street and I win the lottery; I get my big break; I get everything that's coming to me! And you will see my name in the magazines, and you will put my book on the coffee table, and you will hang my art on your wall because my résumé is a masterpiece!

You will say that I am a masterpiece!

But I am not. I'm like you, unskilled in the ways to savvy through AI keywords and sneaky under-table interviews.

I'm not an artist — but I am starving still.

We're Hiring, Please Apply!

seeking entry level gopher right now:
full-time hours every day, in snow or rain
MUST have Ph.D. and <u>blood</u> to vow
our office is suspended by a *crane~*

no benefits for you, benefits us!
know CPR and some scuba diving
please wear a life vest and learn to ADJUST
(did I mention we are conniving?)

professional growth is to be **weeded**
we promise to promote the lazy one
you'll work the jobs where no one's succeeded
unfortunately, your day will never be done

you'll be hired, your future won't be bright...
we will crush your soul to our delight! :)

JOB DETAILS
Required: Ph.D., M.D., J.D., M.A., M.S., B.A., B.S., A.A., A.S.
Location: Hell
Job Type: Indentured Servitude
Compensation: None

Résumé Poem

I'm A Name White People Can Say
123 Please Hire Me Street
You won't regret this, CA 12345
(411) SEE-MEEE
dolphin_dongs@unemployed.com

Skills

Top-notch at google search, efficient as a sinner in church; willing doormat, perfect when your feet are wet; works 26/7, steals time borrowed from heaven; extremely fluent in passive-aggression (uses sparingly, but not excessive)

Education

September 2010–June 2016
B-Tier University, Rural America - Marine Biology, B.S.

Conducted field work with dummy dolphins in the corn groves that faced the Pacific; trained dummy dolphins to "sit" and "stay"; and tied nautical knots to sail the tractor down a river of maize

Experience

my résumé is a jumbled mess; plotted exaggerated success; inexperienced in experience; my lack of skills, I'll never confess

my past employment mysterious; pedestrian work? but serious; me curing cancer, solving world hunger; those who believe are delirious

education first ages me younger; why I applied is a great wonder; making a $100K seemed a good way; I have private loans like a sucker

being a CFO makes good pay; my dolphins are useless, ask away!; my body is willing for the money; my skills are knotty, but I obey!

Languages
Conversational Spanish to order Taco Bell
"We all succeed at the expense of my dignity!"
"No risk, no reward!"

Awards
Best Gopher: Voted Best in Show for Brown Nose
Always Reliable: Pretending that the mortal soul was not sold
#1 Jumper: Always asking "how high?"
Office Sweetheart: Proudly answers to "Hunny Pie"

References
Mom
Childhood Ex-Friend Who Pities Me
Old Supervisor With Only One Brain Cell

Job Hunting Tip Found in Hunter's Digest Weekly

"Job hunt in the morning," Orion says, a strong, sturdy man
camouflaged in a navy-blue suit, brown belt to match brown shoes

He explains his success: "Be born from piss and bullshit;
carry a decoy briefcase; watch out for stray scorpions!"

The Great Hunter whispers a breeze in the grass:
"Do not quiver from the following email notification."

Today, 2:13 A.M.
From: greekgods@jobs.com
To: You
Subject: Greek God Jobs Daily Saved Search Results Today!

> *Top Jobs with Philoctetes University, Adequate College for*
> *Hero Training*
> **34 Manager Jobs in Mt. Olympus, Olympia, Washington**
>   AKA
> 34 Jobs You Don't Qualify For in Mt. Olympus, Olympia,
> Washington

rest sharp-arrowed, narrowed résumé
on forefingers and pull back blind, bowed hope until taut

aim, then fire
repeat, repeat, repeat

until you have staggered and stumbled through thickets of job posting
pages inked in purple hyperlinks

"Make an offering to Artemis," Orion says. "Altar her your organs,
vivisect your intestines, let her feast on your mortal meat."

pray you are in the first 10 applicants, pray your résumé gleams
like the flesh of a fine deer, pray Artemis moves your application
through moonlight

pray she makes your aim true
pray & pray & pray

and when the time is right, pick up the unknown phone number,
answer as if it is the job recruiter

say hello, listen to a breath of silence, and do not hear anything human

"We're calling about your car's extended warranty..."

Daydreams During Rush Hour

Where do you see yourself in five years?

Escalade big corner office,
Gucci rich-city skyline,
Chanel golden-syrupy sun;

I go home before traffic jams like cherry marmalade,
the world pleasant clouds on my shoulders, Balenciaga soft.
Tomorrow, I will have a day at the Ritz-Carlton spa.

Each breath snuggles soma sweet cashmere,
no worries in my yoga poses,
no worries in chef-prepared vegan food.

Picture perfect perfects me,
never needing, only wanting
five years is my land of dreams.

But I wake up, and this question is still here:
"Where do you see yourself in five years?"
I'm supposed to say with you, right here,
with unwashed concrete carpet
and beige mirage furniture.

Perhaps, this is an open office
and I'm supposed to say with family,
and family is you, in the same way family is
a dad who drinks too much, but hasn't gotten that DUI yet.

Perhaps, in five years, I will not be with you,
but be you on the other side of the executive table,
and someone else will be me, answering this question,
stammering a pledge of potential company loyalty
as if this place is a lifeline.

And it is a lifeline working for you,
the premature gratitude I feel,
the chance that maybe you'll pick me,
ask me to be yours, sits so deep in my gut,
anchors me because *what if?*

What if I don't have you in five years,
my wallet empty because I let dreams
and pride keep me afloat,
but we both know I'm gonna drown.

We both know that I'm the fuck-up,
that desperation sticks to me
like an odious perfume in this job interview.
It's the sweat under my arms, under my boobs,
And you can see it in my voice,
you caught the glint of my daydream and I—

Well, we both know you won't hire me,
and I'm going to go a little more hungry tonight,
and my bills are going to be a little more unpaid tonight,
and I will cry because I'm worthless,
I will cry because I can't catch a break,
I will cry as I talk myself out of suicide.

Yet in five years from now,
you're not going to remember me,
but I'll remember you.
I'll remember the way that my college degree
was a shit stain waste of paper.
I'll remember my resentment
as you go home at three in the afternoon.

I'll remember how this was never for me,
I don't have a seat at your table,
I'm not invited to join you,
no matter that your posting says *vacancy.*

Unsolicited DM from High School Classmate

hey hun, heyyyyy! been awhile!
 i was dat gurl from HS
& we were nvr close,
 but we facebook close enuff
~Ur so beautiful~
even tho I nvr said 2 words to u
~Ur so beautiful~
$$$ i am a BUSINESS WOMAN! $$$
i make my own rulez
& i have an opportunity for *YOU*
becuz i prey on da downtrodden
becuz i was preyed upon wen downtrodden.
cum join my cult, cum join my cult
i promise evrytin is ORGANIC.
we make butt plugs plastered from God's penis
u will feel EM.POWER.ED sellin God dicks
their organic, angel gelatin harvested by vegan means;
XXX angels are not animals! XXX
nothing earthly was harmed in making these dildos
idk better, but i will die on dis dildo sword
i will die with butt plugs in my hands
let's get coffee & be parta my team
i'll be ur upline, but i'm no lifeline
i'll watch u drown in private label lube
our lube is made from JESUS tears
pls join my team,
pls join my team
~~Ur so beautiful~
Ur a boss babe, ur da babe
i think ur so [smart/beautiful/gullible]
only smol BIG $$$$$$ to join!
i'll c tmw @ 10:30???

The Application

Please fill out the following questions:
Name
Phone Number
E-mail Address
Upload your résumé here

Click **NEXT** to proceed to the job portal.

Please fill out the following questions:
Name
Phone Number
E-mail Address
Upload your résumé here

Click **NEXT** to continue.

Please fill out the following questions:
High School Education
College/University Education
Work History #1
Work History #2
Skills
Soul

The fragments of your mind cracking under the repetition of these questions, the slices of your shattered sanity as you question if you really need this job. Do you really need this job? Isn't it too difficult to apply? Do you even have the mental energy to complete this application? Wouldn't it be easier to just upload your résumé to Indeed or Zip Recruiter without having to put in any effort? Why should we reward effort? We don't reward effort. Didn't you know it's all a lie? This job already belongs to someone. This is just a formality to ensure that we are considered to be an equal opportunity employer. Everyone is equal here. Everyone is the same with equity, equality, and lies in between.

Call Me Galatea

Tell me about yourself

I am a person, meaning I am human. I have all 10 fingers and all 10
toes. Or maybe not. Maybe a butter knife slipped, and I am a casual
morning toast amputee. I have two parents by virtue of

existence. You can ask if I have a sister or a brother. I can answer
one or none. I went to grade school, and I have a birthday. I can see or
not see depending on the circumstance. I have relevant

experience in what you're seeking. It may also not be relevant to what
you're seeking. I arbitrarily really like dogs and pizza. I do
not eat dog on pizza though. I grew up in places where people

grow up. I am educated in the way people need to be educated.
I breathe in the way people need to breathe. I am blank in the way I
need to be blank. I am empty, virgin in experience, pure in

naivety, but I'm a slut who knows how to beg. Be my Pygmalion. Give
me the identity you think I need. I am polymer clay, ready
to be shaped n' baked at 350 F degrees. I am your Galatea, your

ivory statue, your gopher model, so chisel me useful. I won't
leave you, won't grow to be my own person. I will stay exactly where
you put me, too afraid to ask for a raise. Choose me, craft

me, I'll be faithful Galatea. I'll be your lovely lackey sculpted from
stone. I need no agency except to belong to yours. I will not quit in the
way stone erodes because of shit & spit. I need this

humiliating job. I desperately need you to hire me. Rent and
student loans still exist & my apartment's eviction notice is as binding as
the River Styx.

You Won't Say It

What is your legal name?

Is my name something you can say? Can you pronounce my long vowels and hard consonants? Do I have a glottal stop at the back

of your throat? Can you roll your Rs on the roof of your mouth? Can you read something not in Roman letters? Is Kanji or Cyrillic

too much for your unassuming eyes? Is my name able to cross borders? Does it have a passport that isn't banned from travel?

Or should I just use my *nickname*, my alias like alien, my A.K.A. that's safe for your tongue to say, one that's not too foreign or

made up, one that's good ol' American, the name that fits perfectly with your accent because it's not too different? My

nickname is your safe space for your mouth because when you hear my name, read my name, you go to yourself and say: "I'm

not gonna call you that." Are we talking about that same legal name? The one you deny me, the one you won't use to identify

me, are we talking about that name? The one my mother found beautiful for the nine months I sat in her womb and became

someone worthy and whole, someone whose existence you can't deny because I exist according to my taxes. Are we talking about

that legal, foreign, different name?

Price Check

Last Four Digits of Your Social

The government barcodes babies/ stamps a serialized sequence of
something assigned to us/ like our gender/ pretends to be personalized
like our names/ our digits curl with cruel divinity/ our prices still scan at
the grocery store checkout/ we are more than a social currency stringed
nine numbers long/ we are the sum of our experiences/ of our dreams/
how can you quantify our worthiness when we are infinite possibilities/
the government wants us to be only nine numbers/ but we don't get nine
lives to get things right/ we are lucky if even get to survive.

Assessment Questions

DIRECTIONS:

Read each question carefully.
But you proceed without reading either of these two sentences.
If you're still with me though, I'll tell you a secret.
Don't answer these questions truthfully.
We don't actually want to know anything about you.
Answer these questions like every lying scumbag who made it big.
Leave honesty at the door.
Kill that little truthful angel on your shoulder.
Be the devil it in the details.
Be a devil and more.

External Opinions on Internal Dominions

My previous supervisors would say that my self-discipline is:

a. *Questionable at best.*

> There are days I hunt for the edge of the world, days I want to scavenge my meaning as I walk down sidewalks. I find symphony in crunching leaves under my feet, nature's cymbals shatter into shards. I lose myself in music only I see, an undecided heart thumping wildly. No one commands the strings to play. Gravitas deflates and drags me into a dirge, a treasure map noted with a glass of water, drowning in the sullen bassoon's scream.

b. *Good like drunk math.*

> My self-discipline compares to a B-rated restaurant by the health department. It's not that I don't wash my hands, I just don't wash them as if I'm a surgeon. I run when excited at the pool, splashing tides in a puddle. At times, I hold myself together with duct tape and rubber bands, my bones twist, but nothing breaks. It is the superstition that doesn't work, the Hail Mary at every hut, hut, play. It is the solid bump in the road I pretend is a roller coaster, ignoring the scrape of the undercarriage.

c. *Superior.*

> Perfect DNA from two impeccable pedigrees and years of careful breeding. My self-discipline is God-given: good teeth, no dental work required. Eat only organic vegan meat and wear a simple black T-shirt from Gucci. Has kissed the Queen of England, sired her an heir who is next in line to be King. My self-discipline is the blueprint for plastic surgery's perfect face. Call me Jeff Bezos, call me Bill Gates. I am so rich I made my own currency in Elon rocket ships. I am the standard of beauty, the TikTok algorithm favorite pretty: blonde, blue-eyed, and perky.

Put A Finger Down If

I do not take arguments at work personally:

a. *Mostly true.*

> I don't take work home with me; conversations don't play on repeat in my brain; I don't waste hours thinking of the perfect comeback; I don't act out scenes in the shower because of a work-related matter; I would never let something my boss said
>
> fester like itchy mosquito bites oozing pus because I keep picking at them; blood won't be under my fingernails as the bites scream angry red; I don't remember standing in my manager's office asking for more hours because my mother was sick with stage IV
>
> cancer and she couldn't work anymore; and I don't mind that they said "NO" without listening to me; and I was totally okay when they said that mom would get state disability; and I never held a grudge when they sent me away without a single "Sorry";
>
> and I would never be the type of person to go to the company president's office, sobbing at his doorstep because never before have two grown women left me so broken, their lack of humanity haunting my hollowed steps; and I will never forget the hug
>
> he offered me because he listened; and I would never smile as I heard their names called over the intercom to go straight to his office; and if I happened to get more hours the next day with a $2 raise, I was only a good worker being rewarded accordingly.

b. *Mostly false.*

> I take my work home with me and then I come back the next day ready to stir some shit up.

We Don't Have Villages Anymore

Explain the gap in your employment

This question begets biology, ignores my primordial hips hung stirrup wide as life carves a canyon through my body. My baby, a precious river, erodes who I used to be before her first cry rings

like roaring currents and I know then that my value of existence narrows down to the world I hold in my hands. This question phantoms family, ignores my shriveled belly skin and sagging tits,

refuses to lay offering at the glory my emptied womb, does not pledge loyalty to my progeny, assumes life materializes instantly into being, as if my body is not a treasured temple constructed

eons ago in my foremothers' ovaries. This question errors expectations, ignores my ailing agency and shoves me into weary womanhood, demands me to ripen, pregnant and full, if only I

quell in quiet, if only I do what I am told, assuming I am a fertile field fearful to be salted. But if I am salted, if I am razed to the ground, if I climb out of my pink clam shell and ask to be a pearl,

ask to be more than a gaping canyon, ask to be both daughter and mother, ask to be both birther and worker, then I cannot exist in this space as motherhood. I cannot exist in the eye of the

homemaker's hurricane. I cannot exist in the spine of a corporate company's time with my baby as part of my identity. I will never be human enough with a working womb that only wants to be a

provider, but can't afford the high cost of preschool; and in the years it takes for my baby to bloom, I only receive judgment and questions about why there is a gap in my employment.

Dependent Dependents

My mom has me at 26, got married at 25, knowing that she was pregnant with her first child only two weeks before a wedding that is only remembered in photographs tucked away in the guest room closet. I am not a miscarriage.

My mom and dad make vows to love each other in sickness and in health, for richer or poorer, for better or worse. I'm there in her womb as they say those words, their promises to each other looping around me as if they're there for me too. A little hope resting between them that says things are going to be okay.

They aren't.

       The promises don't stick

&

       I have no memories of them together

married

       as a family.

My mom goes through life walking on the shards of broken promises with a child she didn't plan from a man she didn't want to spend forever with.

My mom gave up her dreams so I could have mine. My mom settled and settled and settled until she found roots in a house more akin to a termite mound than a fruit tree.

I want her to have something to call hers. I don't want her to wake up in the middle of the night in a cold sweat about how she can't pay the bills and I can't help her pay the bills right now.

I was supposed carry us towards a future but I'm 25, too educated, no experience, just a causality in following pre-9/11 thinking. Go to college, pound the pavement, get that money.

Wanna Click My Heels 3 Times

Home address?

Home is where my heart is, but home is not where I live. I use a mailbox at my mom's. No one breaks in and steals my packages. In the Capital of Nowhere, she doesn't got front porch pirates

sulking in lone lamplights under perforated awnings. Is home where I rest my head at night despite, I just want momma to run her fingers through my hair and read me a story like the moms on

TV do? Is it okay that I'm not happy where I live? I have no heart in the house, no soul on the stove. I share it with 3 roommates, we're all cogs in the mediocre machine. I pay rent here, but my

home is 90 miles away down Highway 15. I don't got traditions here. All the food in the fridge doesn't make sense. I can't cook kapusta with frozen chicken nuggets. We can't get pozole from

bagel bites. Home is 3 dogs who lick me to death. Home is looking at a small town and walking into a time capsule. Home is stifling, suffocating, but a familiar handprint. Nothing's changed and I'm

18 again for a weekend. Home is not here, not in this apartment lasagna layered mold and white paint. Not in these four walls, not in bustling city where dreaming ends when it welcomes you in.

Carbon Footprint

Do you have reliable transportation?

Yes.

I will walk two miles in the snow
one way, uphill, to be here.

I will steal a horse from the little girl
next door who got a pony for her birthday.

I will attach rockets to my skateboard,
wear my helmet because safety first.

I will be the LAX jetpack man, hanging out
with airplanes, fly in the middle of the night.

I will take the bus, transfer to the metro,
and then run the last half mile in issued heels.

We All Have 20/20 Vision Until We're Blind in Retrospect

I notice things that others do not notice:

a. *Mostly True.*

> I sit at Starbucks on Bixel and 6th St., cradled by luxury apartments and a poor man's clinic. Across the way, beat-up cars lay, bumpers zip-tied chic and bitchin'. Bougie SUVs worth double my yearly salary roll on by four-wheeled glitzy dipped chipped rims. The leaseholder has no clue if the tire air is considered premium. An unhoused man sleeps under a jutting storefront.
>
> Parking enforcement checks the meters, sunglasses soldering an afternoon glare, ready to smelt every infraction, but they don't realize they aren't the Man, but they are Man enough to ticket you.
>
> A white man wears a Laker's jacket, but not the cheap one with the minuscule logo over the heart. This jacket is deep purple, Royalty Kobe Purple with gold streaming down the arms like gilded rivers, a 24-karat bullseye on his back. He stares at his fuckboi iPhone, no cracks on the screen, and empty iced coffee cubes jingle like coins kept tight in his pockets. He ambles down the nicest sidewalk I've seen in LA for the next twenty feet.
>
> There are no pigeons here, but if you crawl along the afternoon traffic towards Alameda, a man sells knock-off jewelry at a card table, surrounded by glittering diamonds shimmering in actual jewelry stores. Pristine lights shine bright, and I wonder if these are what souls look like when we die.
>
> There are pigeons, but only if you look at the edges of the buildings, flapping in the shadows of refurbished high-rises. Continuous rooftop AC units carry on with a Gregorian chant

that argues with car horns and beautiful women hawking unwanted samples of aloe yogurt as the city's backup choir. A group of high school students cross the street with heavy backpacks aching their shoulders and they wear bright blue uniforms, as if these inner-city kids are bluebloods with silver spoons for braces.

That is, until Skid Row blinks into view. Sunlight pours down gentle warmth atop the heavenly blue tarps, basking in the row of tents and bicycle parts. A dirt-smeared man shares what little he has with the old black woman in the wheelchair, both ragged and weathered, but in this moment together.

The one overnight shelter heaves open her doors, but she's already too full to take more. The Teslas and Lambos don't drive on tiptoe, but race through the streets as if homelessness is contagious, as if giving a dollar or two means liquidating millions. They yell at their GPSs, cursing at the Unhoused Sea who refuses to part.

White pigeons fly up towards
God, the Highest.

b. *Mostly False.*

I look up and the unhoused man is gone, his bed of small tarp and cardboard empty. I should have mentioned that he slept under U.S. Renal Care—Los Angeles Dialysis, but I didn't.

Unawareness is Another Word for Privilege

Isn't it disgusting sometimes how you wish you had other people's tragedies because then you'd qualify for government benefits? Have you all not seen the shambles of this economy?

Can't you just want to fall back into something, slip into social welfare support, just to help you get back on your feet? You don't say this often, but while you have a roof over your head, in the

back of your mind, you know it can be your car. And even then, you know sleeping in a car is considered a luxury, like those people who buy those fancy camper vans, like those people who

shove their family of 10 in a shoebox RV, travel the country, see the sights, enjoy the nomadic life, unaware that so many families sleeping that many people in one space is considered

abject poverty. Unaware that so many kids can't be reunited with their families if there are more than two children per room, unaware that so many people don't thrift for fun, but try their

best to not be made fun of, unaware that so many people can't cook their family three square meals a day, their energy depleted from all work, no play and you sit here, aware & ashamed,

because for a moment you let envy get the better of you. You learn how well the capitalist machine has both failed you and programmed you. Can't despise, can't hate, can't pity the poor

when you and they are on the same side of the window looking in, hoping to get a bit more, but only one of you has time for an existential crisis.

87 Percent of New Military Recruits Are 18-to-24-Year-Olds

Do you claim veteran's preference?

[ ] Yes.

A moment of silence for all the men, for the baby boys barely 18, who fight for freedom at the cost of their souls. Little boys with blood on their hands the moment they graduate bootcamp.

A moment of silence for the boy babies who push up and pull up like buttons on drone strikes and triggers on rifles—every conflict at knifepoint. "We just want to talk," they say, but our hands are held up and we sink to the ground, tremble at a flag with blood and blue lips; white stripes that slice before anyone makes a sound.

A moment of silence for all the boys left broken in a sandbox called Afghanistan; at the swings called Iraq; by the pool of Japan; in the football field of France; in all the places baby boys play. They pretend to kill Nazis in 1942, unaware that Nazis didn't die in Hitler's cyanide; Nazis wear camo green and slip between the rafters of American liberty and dreams; crack open skulls and scoop out brains of little boys just playing a wartime game.

A moment of silence for all the little boys who believe America needs saving; that our nation is helpless. They think America a damsel with wobbly knees and fainting couch off screen. That America needs knights in camouflage to save Her from global monstrosity when it's only Her face blood red in the mirror.

A moment of silence for all the boys, for all the men who lost a limb, who lost trigger fingers and whole legs, who lost years off their lives, divorced their husbands & wives. Left war more villain than hero, left war with more demons than angels, who depreciated in value and America traded them in.

A moment of silence for all the armed women forgotten, their rapes and deaths unaccounted for on military bases. Fort Hood a breeding ground of pain, for no one talks about why women must walk in 2 x 2 formation to gun powder their noses in the little girls' room. Their bodies are another liberty little boys lay claim to.

A moment of silence for the man at the street corner, stained cardboard his only friend, grease and grime his second skin: Homeless vet hungry; please feed me, but no one stops, and the days get shorter. The man sleeps on sidewalks in his silence, of wishing he was a little boy again, wishing he had another way than to follow the blueprint of the American man.

A moment of silence for all the baby boys who can't scrub the blood off their hands. It follows them from overseas; it follows them in their dreams, and baby boys become men on the battlefield. Same hands that once held their innocence as they played in the park. Same hands that grow withered. Same hands that know how to pick a gun apart.

A moment of silence for all the fallen baby boys, for all the lost little girls, for all life taken away from our little world, for our baby boys who lost their souls to fulfill a dream they couldn't comprehend when only 18.

[x] I claim no Veteran's Preference

No Love

Why is there fuzz on a tennis ball?

The tennis ball is the seed of the unexplainable opportunity tree. That green tuft? That fuzz is a coat meant for warmth. In the belly of the bean, in the ball's anatomy, luck sits tight in the radicle—

that's radical! Possibilities tethered in the epicotyl & hypocotyl, waiting to break free of that testa, just don't confuse it with a Tesla, but that glass ceiling is begging to be shattered, to blossom

and bloom; to find new beginnings vis-à-vis stable employment. I want to be bouncy like a tennis ball! Serve me up and whack me across the court, hit me with the full twist of your rotator cuff

in a perfect arc. Your nylon racket should make delicious French fries of my face, all my salty pieces ricochet in every feasible direction, causing mayhem at Wimbledon during a Venus

retrograde. Mom says I become my own opportunity tree, sprout when my luck is down, fuzzy green. I heave myself out of the ground, claw towards the sun with the jagged edges of a Benz'

valet key. Not to be outdone by a badminton birdie that soars playfully in a summer game, I can fly just as high; but, I have the intensity of an offended lady at the country club. My serenity is

synonymous with honking devil geese. According to my father, we are all made from tennis balls, our fuzz money green drenched in greed as the stock market rebounds off the charts. Every broker

named NASD and JONES say we have love in our wallets, but that's another word for nothing in tennis. We're just zero loveless dollars, our game set match with no points. Why is there fuzz on a tennis ball? I don't know, but this brain teaser has my brain all tuzzed And as if this question measured my value, I'd say: the nylon felt slows the ball down as it flies across the court at top speed.

The drag lessens bodily harm should I aim to destroy the other player in their lovely tennis outfit bought at the Ralph Lauren outlet; while I wear baggy shorts and a T-shirt. And to clarify,

I would destroy them. I would communicate their destruction with a rug-burn so fierce as I serve that tennis ball Grinch quick, a torpedo of fuzz, unrelenting to fucking lose when opportunity

demands victory to be in full bloom.

A Glassdoor Review

in this office,
we clock in when the third planet tilts on its axis exactly sixty-nine degrees away from the sun;

in this office,
our morning coffee is pure sunlight, molten and burning, with pesky grounds in the brew again; *god dammit, Karen! You have one job!*;

in this office,
we don't eat breakfast in bed, our beds are right under our desks as we jump up with anticipation and expectations to be breathing our assignments before they even begin;

in this office,
our daily staff meeting is held in a gladiator's pit where the bosses open the gates and let the lions in;

in this office,
we are all yes women because men are too expensive; *Isn't that right, John? Didn't you get that promotion?*;

in this office,
rumors spread fast just like I heard that Alex booty smacked that dude on the fourth floor, you know, that cute mailroom clerk;

in this office,
friendships are as sacred as calling your debt collector back; *Can't you tell? We just love it here*;

in this office,
we are as valuable as an expired coupon the Applebee's waitress doesn't wanna honor;

in this office,
the employee of the month is the same person who the police also dubbed the serial backstabber; *please be on the lookout for this crazy office worker, more at 11, back to you, June!;*

in this office,
your job security is as precious as wet newspaper made for crafting piñatas; your job security is also as sturdy as a smashed piñata;

in this office,
I won't tell you to quit, but I also suggest that you run far, far away; I'm not saying they are holding me hostage, but I forfeited my soul when I signed my contract, so now I'm stuck here;

in this office,
you won't do anything that's in that job description you see online, but you will learn how to commit tax fraud;

in this office, in this office, in this office—

oh, hi mr. boss man,
yes! This is the newest employee, don't she seem sweet?; look at the head on her shoulders, they sure knew what they were doing when they decided to hire this one; yes, yes mr. boss man, of course, sir, don't you know, sir,

in this office, we just love it here.

The Olympians, Keanu Reeves, and Depression Walk Into A Bar

My previous supervisors say that I finish my projects:

a. *Ahead of schedule.*

> I am the Usain Bolt of completion rates. Call me the new Elaine Thompson-Herah. A deadline is just a finish line, and I huff and I puff careful breaths with such efficiency that my shoulders never cramp because my arms are at the perfect ninety-degree angles with my palms wide open here to grab anything worth grasping, and I find the future worth holding, and success is the moan of crossing something off the to-do list.
>
> Michael Phelps and I time ourselves with our speediness. He freestyles and I butterfly stroke my way into turning everything in at least two days early, pre-ejaculate my own cumming, to verify the results are in true accordance with the company policy; I never fail, but I'm known for my overplanning.
>
> Procrastination? I don't know her, sounds like they dope her. Sounds like she was banned from competing, can't succeed when you're caught cheating, but not me, not me, not when I'm so hardworking. And here's a copy of my five-year plan, color coordinated, scented for all your senses, and you can make sense of the cents I left floating in the margins to ensure there are no more surprises in the budgeting.

b. *On time.*

> I am always where I am meant to be. The entire universe keeps me as I need to be kept, my life as fortunate as a fortune cookie. I am lotto lucky; I am no sweat, baby; I get what I need; when I ask, life provides in the way life does, aligns my chakras, keeps my spirit fresh n' whole, sends Keanu to mentor my dreams.

I am unperturbed with the befores and the afters, only looking in the now, only basking in what I can do, never worrying for the sake of worrying, never doubting for the sake of doubting, but enjoying the steps, the process, the take my time and I will always arrive looking picture perfect, arrive on time, arrive in present tense, here to stay, here to be. Oh look, here's the promised project I said would be done by three.

c. *I am chronically behind schedule.*

I want to say it's a disease that I can't turn anything in on time; name it depression, call it anxiety, diagnose me with executive dysfunction, but I must surely enjoy the thrill of staying up late the night before I fall like Icarus into the sea, my wax wings melting useless things, my brain only borrowing clichés in the time crunch, my mind no longer spinning in originality. I must like wearing disappointment like a moldy fur coat, out of season and out of style. I must like being a disappointment. I must like hearing the sighs, the regrets and watching my relationships tear like stretched, scabbed skin, ripping in half due to my inability to pin my reliability, to keep my promises in what I say to you.

Tardiness and missed deadlines must be some of my favorite lovers, because we get so high together, ignoring responsibilities as if Black Death is upon us once again, choking me, killing me, keeping me breathless, making it hard to suck in the oxygen I need, but there are not enough Plague Doctors to douse me in flowers to cure me, to help me, to save me as I suffocate in the mess that bears my body for my timeliness.

Marilyn Monroe Interviews for Corporate

Why do you want this job?

I want to say this eloquently,
like Lincoln's address at Gettysburg,
like Churchill in the House of Commons,
like Q on every 4Chan posting,
but fatherfucking money, honey.

I want you to jackhammer pound
your Gs into my checking account
and our eyes lock dollar signs in the mirror
and payday orgasms a shopping spree
at Target instead of anything secondhand.

I want to be dainty,
a real little lady,
giggling sweet
behind a pale pink manicure
hiding a coy smile,
plumping and pumping
my lips in anticipation.

Tell me your name is Benny,
give me some sweet & sexy
healthcare, dental, and vision,
wine n' dine me on vacation packages,
twirl me, whirl me about some mythical
pension and if you're feeling really saucy,
whisper to me about all the stock options.

When Jobs Don't Ask for SnapChat

Best number to contact you

Do you promise to call me? I don't have time for the will you/won't you telephone game, don't want no voicemails found

in the retired missed connections of a Craigslist posting. We are not exclusive, but I want to be. If I give you my 10 digits, area code

and all, and promise it's not for a prank service, will you call me? Hit me up for an interview where I make sweet love to you with

all my experience? Can you do that? Will you call me? We can even do it over the phone, I can operate all communication.

I'm told my customer service voice is oh so pleasing. Baby, you can even text me all your eggplants, all your tacos—hell, I'd be

even happy to see an infinite row of octopi. Sext me, text me at 2 A.M., give me directions on how to best send a fax. Ask me out,

ask me about all my friends, tell me to work overnight and to never clock in. Send me your lat and lon to somewhere in remote

Alaska and I'll parachute out of a plane to land on your postage-stamp-sized lake. Tell me when, tell me how—give me directions

where to put my impressive self, inside your garage. Do you cover parking?

Security! They Misunderstood the Question

Sex: Male or Female

I got aspirations in my pants &
my private parts are a gateway to my heart.
I want you to slip n' slide between my thighs,
crack me open like a cold one with the boys.
Go down under and enjoy my thunder,
my cheeks are butterball turkeys—
big and delicious, maybe even a little buttery.

Don't be shy, King, Queen, Your Majesty,
you propositioned me!
You wanted to know my F or my M,
wanted a peep at what's underneath,
wanted to tickle a tip to my P or my V,
wanted to know if we can make a baby.
Do we got the right jump drive and USB,
do I got the parts that you need?
Is this not a question of my biology?
Does my sexual compatibility
predetermine my skills as an employee?
Do eggs or sperm spell Manifest Destiny?

All I got is ambition and I'll give it to you good.
All I am is begging and prepping, ass up, eyes closed.
Take me Daddy, step on me Mommy.
You'll never meet anyone as thorough, I aim to please,
my dignity left forgotten on the commute's breeze.
So, yes, yes, boss baby, sex me up, touch me here,
just promise I'll get that five percent raise every year.

Under the Bus

My previous supervisors would describe my ability to work well with others as:

a. *Superior.*

> I am friendly to a nauseating degree. I am the germs from the sneeze that fell into your mouth. Once we come in contact, you're infected by me. Unable to escape as I ravage your immune system, taste the tip of your nerve endings, feast on your pleasant plasma.
>
> Your T-Cells know my fingerprints and give me access to all your vulnerabilities, and I find a home in your genomes, lounging comfortable in your lungs, as you hack up your hesitations.
>
> We might be colleagues, but I slip inside your papercuts, breathe under your bandages until I seal myself into the scab. Can I become the scar you don't want anyone to see? You might be a lone wolf, but I am a viral duplication until we are a pack, until you are defenseless, breathless, weak and wrecked savaged.
>
> Call me a parasite as I sneak into your skin, as I implant myself into the best parts of you, take hold of your heartbeat and wait there, resting only to have you flatline, after I've finished all there is to eat, after I've tapped you empty, after I tell you, in your final moments, as you're marched to the feverish firing squad.

b. *Average.*

c. *Below Average.*

> There is no "I" in TEAM, but if you rearrange the letters, you'll learn to not @me and this is the truth, so don't you know I don't like you anyway? Don't you know you mean nothing? Don't you know that trust is a trick, and you should know better than this?

C'mon, girl, can't believe you thought this all wasn't a game; can't believe you didn't feel my boots digging into your skull as I scaled your spine, your bones a good ladder for me to climb higher, your body pliable, flexible.

I twist you and your words & bend you over backwards & pretend and pretend and pretend. Don't you see the casting couch? Don't you know we're all fucked in the way none of us want to get fucked? But if I have to take it and cry a little, I don't want to sob alone anymore.

Rumors Say You Liked Him

Tell me about a time you had a conflict with a co-worker

You had a co-worker who always told you were the most beautiful woman in the room. He was your friend, though, in the way men can be your friends. He said your eyes shone like the brightest stars. He would try to pillow into your bosom, his eyes so sleepy.

Sometimes you now wonder if it's your fault, because you used to laugh at the dirty jokes. Sometimes you wonder if your laughter was an unwilling invitation crossfaded with acceptance, but can you dine n' dash flattery?

Shouldn't you have been thankful for the way he leered at you when you bent over to gather the papers he dropped? Weren't you both just being team players? Wasn't this another word for comradery?

He would invite you anywhere, all the time. Midnight, he would text you. *Hey, want to grab something to eat? It's Saturday night. Let's get some drinks.* You exchanged numbers to work on a group project, but your project was always just him and you. It seemed so harmless, all the coffee, all the food.

It seemed absurd, the way his kindness turned your stomach sour. Sometimes he would speak for you, as if he knew what you wanted. Sometimes he would decide for you, as if he knew what you wanted. But friends mean well, don't they?

You had a co-worker touch you when no one was looking. It started at your shoulder, to the base of your neck, until his mouth stole your choice in a clandestine hallway.

You told him "no!" but he heard yes. You said "stop!" but he heard more. You yelled "let me go!", but he heard *fuck me, darling. Fuck me, fuck me, darling.*

In the aftermath, your supervisor didn't believe you when you told him what happened. Human Resources only sneered and said: "Can't reprimand him just because you're a loose girl and have regrets." The policeman only looked at you and shook his head.

You had a co-worker love you without your consent. You had their fingerprints bruised on your skin. You had a job once, but you had to quit.

They say tape tastes better over plundered lips. Isn't it better to just solve conflict with silence?

National Geographic Did Not Sponsor This Poem

I watched a documentary once that said Human Resources works something like 9 to 5 on that daily grind, living that Monday through Friday life.

Another scientist came on screen and refuted that claim, said that Human Resources only worked 7 to 3:30 on Tuesdays that rained.

The scene changed to a woman answering a rotary phone suited in JCP's black and white finest, big bargain bags bellied under her eyes: "This is Disappointment. If you're looking for Recruitment, they've changed their name to *Talent Acquisition*."

I remember sitting on the couch, popcorn in my hand, this documentary shifting into a Charlie Chaplin silent film, but I don't remember laughing.

A number flashed across the screen so I called to see if I could get a job at JCPenney. The busy signal blared long after the credits played.

Not All Birds of a Feather Flock Together

How would your last manager describe you?

"No good for nothin'
lazy-ass millennial,
entitled little girl."

sees my mouth as a dull beak,
hears my voice as Twitter feed,
sees me as no one, calls me nobody,
won't say my name Odysseus.

just a little girl, baby-faced
parasitic worm, squashed under her shoe.
"no good for nothin'
lazy, unremarkable entitled child"

child like her children,
like her husband's mistress' children.
lost little cowbird, lost little brood;
squawks as if I am fluent in crooked rook,
fluent in the knife play of her wood pecking Morse code.

if only she knew I give her flight,
that she glides on my breath;
my breeze dances in her awarded wings.
I inhale all her chaotic demands,
exhale a flock of starling reviews;
migrate us to tomorrow with no smoke.

if only she can see how I rustle the leaves,
if only she could stop seeing green,
maybe then she could hear the gust in my gales,
can say "thank you" for her oxygen,
can say "thank you" as she heads south for the winter.

she mockingjays the screeching kettle,
but I don't speak steam.
I only stream through the day unseen,
pollinating the workflow, multiplying success.
without me, the earth won't turn,
the work stacks mountain high, avalanche ready.

at the peak, where the atmosphere thins,
clarity chirps in breathless vulnerability.
she calls me into her nested office
long after the flock goes home;
pours me some Wild Turkey,
pecks her lips amongst the glass and says:

"you and me,
we're zephyr divine.
'yes ma'am, yes sir' kind of people.
we carry things that fly,
expectations snowpack us in a storm
of liquid white paper, buries us
in a sea of Amazonian bones."

she says this sparrow soft,
sighs a despondent whistle.
the clock strikes the hour,
each second a flutter's wingbeat
as she peers into her whisky amber.
her feathers molt in her glass,
pooling her reflection like a mirage,
unable to recognize she's a cuckoo bird.

Monologue From My Unemployed Boyfriend

baby, the e-mails are repeating; a torrent hurricane of rejections sting like wild wasps; *dear applicant, we've selected another candidate*;

baby, you smile as if you're the sun, as if the moment I see you in dawn's whisper kiss before you go to work will be enough; I only open my eyes a sliver to crack my dreams as day sneaks into our bedroom to remind you where you left your favorite earrings; they're on the nightstand hidden by your water cup; the tension in my spine melts as you press your lips to each part of my vertebrae in your goodbye;

baby, I steal your pillow, your love as refreshing as the cool side; I pretend your scent wets my parched soul as I try to discern my true calling for fulfillment;

baby, I text you asking for money, my pockets empty wells; I used to buy you dinners, and we each got our own desserts; I never liked sharing, never wanted to give you the last bite of factory cheesecake;

baby, I'm so grateful you let me have the last bite of your favorite chocolate chip cookie from your company's meeting lunch today;

baby, you never make me beg, but I want to buy that new video game, see the colors explode as my character runs across the screen; I close my eyes and I am the hero for a moment; grass crunches under my feet and dust clings to my clothes; I don't want to go outside; I slept too long anyway; I've wasted my whole day;

baby, you give me the grocery list and I am lost in the decisions that I have to make between name-brand and generic items; you asked for frozen snow peas, but I hiked to the tallest freezer; there was none. you told me to get fresh ones; *baby*, I had to ask you where and you said the produce section with such clarity I thought I should've seen the yellow brick road to common sense with you;

baby, my résumé stares at me with a blank page, my experiences blaring sirens of inadequacy, my confidence crumbles with every new job posting; I should have done more, but I am drowning; dad forgot to teach me how to swim; unproductivity tastes like flat soda from last night, sounds like dirty dishes in the sink I didn't do again; the leaning tower of pots crashing like a cymbal in the symphony's coda;

baby, I'm not a work of art, I am no masterpiece; you come home after a long day, purple under your eyes, weary bones; and I am afraid of my e-mails, stuck in cement as you have to continue for the both of us; I can't even do the dishes like I promised;

baby, I want to love you, but it hurts to love you right now; I am living in the shadow of our dreams, hollowed out by the potential of where we could have been in our five-year plan; we can't even afford our own house now; baby, can I have gas money again? Is it okay if I go out to lunch?;

baby, baby, baby, are you sure you want to stick with me?; what if no one else finds me to be good enough?; how can you be so sure I'm the right one?; we've made no vows to each other, but you act if I stop breathing then you will too, as if our lungs are one, as if I am your oxygen.

baby, the e-mails are repeating; dear applicant, we've selected another candidate; but baby, I want to love you as if you are my oxygen; baby, you are my oxygen; you are my everything; you are the cure to my insecurities; if only for a moment; if only for a breath; but to me, despite I am nothing, only you can be my eternity.

baby, can you look over this application before I send it in?

Money Hungry

money hungry is not the same as being greedy; it's just having no stress, having enough that all our needs are met, having a rainy-day jar actually makes sense

money hungry is when my mother wonders how she's gonna pay the mortgage; where we search in between couch cushions for loose change and I just want to change our situation, but even my college degree is only worth pennies

money hungry is me as I sit here barely making more green than the poverty line, but I'm drowning in student debt with interest at 10.25% doing only as I was told; however, the red line of my bank account sees no difference

money hungry is wanting decent conditions and to have enough, to be enough as is, where we sleep at night in a good bed, those damn dollar signs don't follow us to dreamland

money hungry is when we glorify poverty as if it is prosperity, consume movies about how poor heroes are million-dollar stories, where rags to riches can only be a thing of fiction when I'm just left yearning to win two bucks off a lotto ticket

money hungry is the natural state of human existence crumbling and withering under our capitalist system that doesn't care about our benefits or well-being; when our end is a means to some CEO's faux budgeting

money hungry is another word for starvation salivating for the future to be delivered sooner, where my hunger is satiated on my

financial security, and where I have money to finally open that account for retirement savings

A YouTube Ad from the Grassroots Campaign

Foresting skyscrapers, canopy glass dreams
Dreams a myth of worker bees
Bees a reality, honey the wealth
Wealth a rich promise never seen
Seen at sunrise over smoggy peaks
Peaks crescent on apartment buildings
Buildings knotted in uprooted contracts
Contracts a clawed conversation
Conversation another word for survival
Survival the law of living
Living requires not poverty in the city

City, the jungle, city, the land
Land weeps under concrete
Concrete did not ask to be broken
Broken gravel and grit mix into shackles
Shackles ache to birth green grass
Grass aches for deer teeth
Teeth a consequence for trying
Trying a consequence for existing
Existing a brief moment for something more
More than tamed nature under suffocating propaganda

Propaganda shines as bright as the sun
Sun only a lightbulb in the sky
Sky a ceiling where our hands touch the limits
Limits a lie that says we are cherished
Cherished is what I call a conglomerate
Conglomerate a group of different things, say corporations
Corporations a creature with more rights than me
Me, a person, who is only to work, never want
Want, a desire to live with no needs and only peace
Peace a wish I have under foresting skyscrapers

Skyscrapers a prison where I never sleep
Sleep the enemy of company profit
Profit the enemy of people
People never knowing that life is not meant to be echoed
Echoed is all we are taught when we think
Think is another word for dream
Dream is a glass canopy
Canopy is a forest I will never see

See how I do not know how to fight for myself
Myself does not know how to fight for breath
Breath is something money does not need
Need is all I am comprised
Comprised to ask for water and something to eat
Eat is what my mother tells me when I come home
Home is precarious in this economy
Economy is another word for ecosystem
Ecosystem is a network of mutual benefits
Benefits none of us has seen since who knows since when
When was the last time we were actually human?

My Therapist Says I'm an Anxious People Pleaser

I really want to get things right all the time:

a. *Agree.*

> Perfection requires attention. Constant vigilance. Always looking over my shoulder. Failure hunts like a biped, orbital cavity at front of skull. Hunts with steady steps; moves forward; never tires.
>
> I doubt it's panacea to cure all ailments. Failure comes back stronger after mending broken bones. I run on all fours, ungraceful and in fear.
>
> Keep running, keep running. Constantly out of breath, exhaustion sags my skin. I trip, scrape my elbows and knees. I bleed disappointment in my wet wounds and Failure's lips smack with salivating anticipation.
>
> Failure's steady walk shifts into a monstrous crescendo. Perfection holds vigil in the horizon's setting sun. Sharp fangs nip at my calves. Failure's breath trickles a miasma with an open maw.
>
> Drool dribbles on my split skin. A warm mouth tongues me whole; I'm smashed amongst Failure's teeth. Echoes of my screams slide down Failure's wet, sloppy guzzling throat.

b. *Neither agree nor disagree.*

c. *Disagree.*

> I want to pretend that I don't care about getting things right on the first try. I am a trained dog, though. I want to be told "good girl". I want someone to pat my head, rub behind my ears, and give me a treat. I know better than to trust the palm that reaches out to me.

I snap and snarl; I foam at the mouth, bubbles spitting tidal waves. My teeth click fierce when Perfection gets too close. I know it's not real. I'm not a "good girl" so I get locked outside in the barren yard. I am filthy in the dust and dirt. I am filthy. I jump and scratch at the sliding door, but the TV volume only gets louder.

So, I bark, rabid and hoarse, but all you hear is: "I don't care about being perfect."

If you spoke dog, you'd hear: "Please let me be good enough."

But you don't speak dog, so, you reply: "Someone shut that damn bitch up!"

Papers, Please

Are you a U.S. Citizen?

Is this a trick question? Am I inviting xenophobia into my life? Will you tell me to go back to where I came from if I answer otherwise?

Do I have to be American to be part of the economy? Isn't this the land of dreams? Of freedom? Wasn't this land snatched away from other hands? What are citizenship and personhood to a nation of invaders who paved the way for Indigenous slaughter?

For how long do I have to be a citizen? Does it start and end only with me? Do I need to tell you my family history? What if I have memories of another country?

What if my family came across the sea on a rickety ship stuffed to the brim? One by one, only scraps of skeletons knitted together in the aftermath of concentration camps rest in the belly of a boat we can't translate into English.

What if their fingers skimmed the waves as they sailed to somewhere new because they could not keep all their limbs inside? What if they came here with pickled fingers, all pruned up and useless due to the sea's brine? What if the oozing wound of World War II dyed the Atlantic red from peasants who couldn't read or write?

Is my family the sort of citizens you want? The type that was left to rot. Is my lineage going to be acceptable to you? Will you hold it against me that I haven't been here since Plymouth Rock and helped the Pilgrims spread disease?

Am I American enough with just dreams?

A Story from the Timeline I Still Spoke Ukrainian

Are you fluent in any language other than English?

I speak in the tongues that got me bullied on playgrounds; I use my mouth to tell my mother I love her and Welcome Home; in the same language where my accent wasn't good enough.

My language has been discussed in legal meetings: "Can we make all employees speak English, so no one feels left out?"

I've been left out of conversations before I could talk. My place to speak interrupted by twisted faces, brows furrowed with ridges, wrinkled foreheads and pursed lips that don't know what it means to be part of the legacy born in a concentration camp.

I am left lonely trying to explain an idiom that doesn't translate into English. I am left lonely in the aftermath of salted fields English pillaged from my mouth, taking my words, and wringing out the passion.

Yes, I am fluent in something other than English. It's the same way I know how to keep my mouth shut when you speak to me. The same language that doesn't want to explain my first name.

You look at me as if I'm only a dictionary. You look at me as if I am quota enough for the diversity you need, that my mouth can make up for all the languages in the world as its representative. That my mouth can speak for countries because we share the same foreign root language. My voice cannot speak for everyone you're afraid to hear.

Ode to the Migrant Worker

thank you for coming,
are your feet tired?
you've come so far.
let me tend your hands,
palms flesh pink,
skin drenched in sun.
are you hungry?
I've prepared the fruits
of your labor on my table.
strawberries, apples, melons,
peppers, tomatoes;
here are the fresh eggs and milk,
fine beef and fish. let me
take care of you, let me feed you,
let me shower you like summer crops
that need the rain.
oh, dear worker, sweet farmhand,
let me take my country
off your shoulders.
you only need to carry
your own spine after dark.
shall I run a bath for you?
can I wash your hair, pick stray grass out
of the wind swept tangles? let me love you,
heroic migrant worker, if only for a moment,
until America forgets again, let me thank you.

Based on a True Story

I feel uncomfortable around people who are different than me:

a. ~~Mostly True~~.

b. *100% false.*

> I pick up the phone to answer a customer:
> "Help Desk. How can I help you?";
> she thanks me for speaking English;
> I say "I don't understand";
> she tells me that not all my co-workers speak English;
> I should know what she means;
> she says they don't speak English
> the way that she and I speak English;
> she says we speak English with a point of privilege;
> we are people born to put our hands over
> our hearts because we see a flag;
> she says we speak English with good values;
> we like simple food and mom and pop shops;
> we speak English in the same way
> we like celebrating Thanksgiving;
> the Indians were only helping the Pilgrims;
> she says we are good people;
> we cross the street and tug our purse tight to us
> when we see young brown men walking;
> the Civil War was fought to free slaves;
> it's not rude to call people Oriental;
> she says she means ornamental;
> and yes, all Asians look the same;
> don't you agree?;
> she says wow,
> I didn't realize you liked ethnic food;
> seasoning salt is too spicy;
> it's un-American for that black man to be kneeling;
> we just want peaceful protests;

she says all lives matter;
of course it was those people
who decided to loot and riot;
we speak English because we are monolingual;
we speak English and—;
I interrupt her and I say:

i. "All my co-workers speak English, ma'am."

ii. Her voice crackles like privilege before her: "But they
have—" (accents; foreign names; brown skin)

iii. "All my co-workers speak English, ma'am. All of my
co-workers are human, ma'am. All my co-workers are
intelligent, clever, diligent people, ma'am. All my co-workers
speak goddamn English, ma'am. All my co-workers—" My
chest heaves, my voice rises, my face reds and— "We are
all just people, ma'am! Now this is Help Desk, how can I
fucking help you?"

    Click.
    Click.
    Click.

iv. I look up and realize my supervisor pressed disconnect, the
line rings dead in my ear. "We don't need to talk to people
like them," he says. He points to the sign tucked away in a
corner. "We have the right to refuse service."

Robot Overlords

How do you think technology advances will impact your job?

Let's start from the beginning:
the Big Bang, the Mesozoic Era, the Ice Age,
Niles and Euphrates cradling Mesopotamia, cradling Egypt,
the Indus River Valley a vibrant song, building the Great Wall,
the fall of Xeres's Persia, Alexander the Fucking Great,
a mirage of stone, iron, bronze, silk roads,

Marco Polo, Holy Crusades,
The Black Plague, Christopher Columbus,
Guns and Steel, Guns and Butter, Guns and Boats,
White Man and Genocide & Genocide & Genocide,
the Native Americans fed the Pilgrims,
the Conquistadors, the Slave Trade,
Manifest Destiny, Lewis and Clark, the Alamo,
the Mexican-American War,

a house divided will fall apart,
the lightbulb, the telephone,
the assassination of Franz Ferdinand,
World War II, Nazi boots,
my family in a concentration camp,
my family part of the Sea of Japan,
atomic bombs, atomic bombs,
Civil Rights, Black Panthers, White Power,
Vietnam, napalm, Agent Orange, Roe v. Wade,
burning bras, working moms

the internet, a turn of a century,
a turn of two centuries,
a turn of a millennium,
JT and Brittany in matching jeans,
Iraq, Afghanistan, the Taliban, Daesh and Syria,

suicide bombers, Parkland Shooting, Russia invades Ukraine,
and we are still stuck in slow motion,
supply chains broken,
a pandemic repeating history,
again, again, again
&
I am in a race towards extinction,
my every exhale forewarned obsoletion
stuck in death oscillating lifetimes of deletion,
her Scythe a farmer's sickle,
a soldier's machete, a policeman's knee,
a piece of bent electric wiring, a CPU, a motherboard,
an echo of Eve's apologetic hands calloused by burying Abel,
an echo of the lepers at Jesus's feet,
mirroring, manifesting Skid Road in Los Angeles,
manifesting next day shipping,
coding a new Gospel heralded by Siri
sanctifying a bright, delicious Apple,

and I bow my head in prayer,
my phone the new Bible,
the Algorithm my God,
Divine Intervention feeds me,
and I don't have to wonder
if my AI Savior hears me late at night,
when I unravel the infinite scroll,
sliding my thumb in penance, in breath,
in history at my fingertips,
but I wait for the targeted ad about a shower speaker
I said I wanted once, embraced in advertisements
like clergy stoles, like Archangels in the night,
my ideology, a teaching delivered via push notifications,

and in this new electric landscape,
this new mass extinction event
of melting Polar Ice Caps,
of drought riddled lands,
of human disconnection,
I trust that the metaphysical
is only my body and my blood,
my reality only mine through my eyes,
I break my bread,
I sip my wine,
I am my own truth,
hypoxic automated suffocation another way to say:

Alexa, Siri, oh Glory to the Highest, ChatGPT, query: how can I
worship the robot overlords?

A Bitter Barista's Brew

dear customers,
a barista is not a magician,
not a magic man with magic hands,
cannot spindle coffee from your spittle,
cannot brew a blonde roast
beautiful into your demanding wishing cup,
cannot use telekinesis to siphon Frappuccinos
and lattes onto your tongues.
that's how you get a lawsuit.

dear customers,
a barista is not a punching bag,
not a target painted bullseye red,
cannot stand there still for your aim,
cannot wait your tantrum out
over a well-needed price check,
cannot call off your demons when you have a bad day.
that's why people have therapists.

dear customers,
a barista is not the lucky one in this situation,
not the chosen one,
cannot save you from yourself,
cannot give you all of life's answers as if they know the answer,
cannot bless you as if they are beings giving out blessings,
cannot rub their tummies like baby buddhas—
that's just racist.

dear customers,
a barista is just a barista,
some poor person who loves coffee
enough to hate themselves
to make it on a daily basis;
because that's what happens when you're passionate,
you turn into a masochist.

but dear customers,
this is not a BDSM scene,
you do not get to dominate just because baristas
often get on their knees
to wipe the showcase clean.
that's how customer service works.

dear customers,
I got another job, bitches.
you losers are worth nothing, not worth the bank fee
when I over drafted, not worth the stress
of five a.m. drive-thru openings, but my God,
it feels nice to spit in all your coffee even at the cost
of a bioterrorism felony.

please die in a fire,
signed from your local former barista,
with all my love,
me.

An Actress's Anecdote Scribbled on a Blog Post

I am an actress,
eyes bright, hair shiny,
fresh perkiness as bitter burnt coffee.

"Hello!
Welcome!
No need for a reservation!"
The script notates that I speak from my diaphragm,
project my voice from the first row to the sidewalk entrance;
today I star as your doting waitress.

I break the leg, step forward to my audience,
I show you to your table,
"Here's the corner booth you requested!"
I recite our daily specials
with the reverence I no longer reserve for Shakespeare,
the sun blaring through the window like stage lights.

A kid asks for crayons, their sticky hands gum the table and
I am reminded that Broadway is only a cross street in Chinatown
and my theater is only a packed pancake house.

But ravenous ambition licks my ribs
and resentment flares like a gas stove
under my sternum scarcely contained by a pleasant smile.

My voice void of dripping viciousness as I repeat your order,
as if this moment is worthy of an encore:
Am I an actress?
Stuck here with diner grease as my costume,
consumable American culture stuck at the back of my throat?

I exist in the same suspended reality
where I fight with gravity and the gallows,
praying for a moment where I become someone else.

I am meant for Broadway, to be the lead in every play,
I have eaten every line, know the taste of each inflection.

Juliet's "O! Romeo," is floral as her rose,
Ophelia's grief drowns me in acidic bitters,
Lady Macbeth's lies layer luscious chocolate cake.

Today I'm a stage waitress,
my big break as small as the pennies left on my tables,
my only lines are when I have more than two customers waiting.
This is not what I want but daydreams are not enough.
Aren't I an actress?

but—

"Hello!
Welcome!
No need for a reservation!"

No Rest for the Working

Describe your biggest weakness

I am tired—dripping, drooping, exhaustion caught in gravity's fatigue, dragging me down deep, far from sleep's reach. I am tired.

My brain never quiets, never silent, never lulls to lullabies I sing, never rests in the respite of rooibos tea, never stills, never chamomile calm cupped comfort strong enough for sleep to come. I am tired.

I am tired in the way I work hard, not smart, but harrowing through heaps of hellish humps, bumps, jagged messes I should not have to clean, the deadlines deadly apparently to everyone but me, so I am left as the decision maker, the doer, the driver who never gets to sleep in the passenger seat. I am tired.

My joints ache, the ligaments of my limits longing to lollygag, my body's expiration souring milk in the sun, but I pray that I will be enough, that in my lame lethargy, I can override my human biology and evolve to be a robot, an android, an automaton, to be made of iron, to be made of circuit boards and software in all the hardest parts of me. I am tired.

I am tired, but my lack of rest keeps me between prosperity and poverty; keeps my pantry piling packaged packets for rainy days; keeps the roof over my head and gives my belly something to eat. I am tired.

My body is weak, but I am strong enough, I promise, to do what's asked of me, to be the person who jumps through all the hoops and looks pretty. To be the one who does not need sleep. Afterall, sleep is for the weak.

I am tired.

Only Doing What I Was Told, Sir

When crunched for time, it's acceptable to cut a few corners:

a. Always.

>Supervisor tells me to get the job done verbally, refuses to use a paper trail. Do this, *grunt cunt*, do this now. Slides a list of deadlines in the space between their words, as if Supervisor is afraid to say this out loud, knows a rule and how it breaks. Handbook rests under used coffee mugs, stained with spilled red ink as Money Bags Boss Man shouts demands behind his office's closed doors.

>Supervisor tells me to get the job done, potential promotion presses sharp into my spine, a warning flaring in a shallow cut. Deadlines ring with every phone call in worker bees' hall to make things happen when no one knows what's happening. I crick-crack my neck, trigger finger quick—a reverberating metaphorical gunshot echoes in my ear as my shoulders square themselves thick.

>I take a stack of petty cash without counting all the bills.

>I do not use our approved vendors, don't follow the guidelines etched in my eyeballs. I do not ask for permission and I know there will be no forgiveness.

>I bully my way through the red-tape, soft silver tongue sly when an uptight co-worker asks what I'm doing. I remember the rulebook under used coffee mugs, and I direct them to the breakroom to mind their own damn business.

>Deadlines beep like frighten bombs as Money Bags Boss Man shouts like a thundering toddler, roaring demands and my potential promotion licks me into a fire. Supervisor tells me to get the job done so, I swindle my way to 100%.

b. *Sometimes.*

c. *Never.*

I would never admit to cutting corners — knowing the rulebook full well on which procedures I can bend, but I'm not stupid enough to select answers A or B.

Dear Mr. Bossman

The warranty has expired on our relationship,
you've put nails in all my tires.
My check engine light
has been on for the last three thousand miles
and you never got back to me
if I had to work all of Fred's double shifts.
I come in here with motor oil
pouring out of my pores,
bending in the same way as a broken control arm,
but I am sick of giving you control.
I don't need you to steer me
in any direction, there is no power left
for you to guide to me.

Mr. Bossman,
don't you see,
the lease of us has ended,
we have gone all our miles
and my tank is running empty.

It's you,
it's definitely you
as to why I'm quitting,
as to why we,
why you and me,
are a total loss.

Accidents happen in the same vein
you need to change your filters,
you need to buff out all the scratches
to your person because you are looking
like a used junk car the more the days go by.

Mr. Bossman,
you're a head-on collision
who doesn't follow the traffic lights,
you missed the green arrow
and now you're stranded in the intersection
with your pants around your ankles.

Mr. Bossman,
I need an upgrade,
I need something new,
something sleeker
and more fuel efficient
that's better for the economy.
All I know is that I don't need you.

Please don't ever contact me,
Me

Pack Animal

I do not like for people to rely on me:

a. Mostly true.

I want

- to arrest time,
  prison its concept into the void;
- blood vessel violins stroking a concerto in my ears;
- satiation & rest, peaceful, dripping tea from my
  humid breath;
- solitude to rotate my axis, sunning myself
  in my own galaxy.

In these

- new cosmos;
- sweet oblivions I call mine,
  I water only myself in my new world.

My

- joy becomes the sun, pours gold in my cup;
- sorrow pours the rain, washes my shoulders from
  hard work;
- work sprouts only for me.

I want

- to not wear the caretaker's hands;
- if only for a moment, if only for a breath, to be
  selfish.

b. *Mostly false.*

> I am a rectangle,
> solid and leaned-lined,
> covered in gray,
> trusty elephant hide;
> Rest under my shade
> that kisses the countryside;
> Call me America's Heartland
> who holds the solar star up
> with my hands for the morning's sunrise,
> ready to plow the fields and harvest the grain.
>
> I am the ebb and flow,
> beat and breath
> of time moving,
> humming steady perfection
> in the way I shoulder your worries.
>
> I weave freesias into your hair,
> knot the flowers strong so none fall out.
> I will take care of you when the hurricane gallops
> from coast to land and the levees break.
>
> I will float,
> treading violent
> and unpredictable waves
> as I keep your head above water.

A Twitter Thread Tagged #GoFundMe

I'm losing my job tomorrow. I thought I wasn't gonna care, this place is a literal hellhole, but sometimes hellholes are cozy.

I'm losing my job tomorrow, but I closed the shop with care, I said goodbye to my favorite customers, and I wonder where's my despair?

Employment has no room for me, jobs never want to hold me close, and I know that, I know that deep in my bones.

I wish I wouldn't lose my job tomorrow; my car payment is due on the 10th. Can I move enough money around so that feels less like a hit and more like a dent?

If you can, please donate to my #GoFundMe page? It's all I got to live. If I knew how to art, I'd draw you some porn, but right now, all I can do is beg to hold on a little longer.

Warning: Background Check

*Have you been convicted of a crime (a felony or a misdemeanor) in the
last seven years?*
>   —as answered by a cousin

You look at my résumé and only see poverty, only see the projects with
fireworks as gunshot lullabies.

You wonder about a sun-damaged car with an unpainted bumper and
ponder about plastic vinyl dress shoes and an ill-fitting suit.

You search for the bodega in my belly, try to calculate the value of all my
free meals from the school-lunch program, and estimate

the negative returns of your wasted tax dollars. Yet I'm here now tattoo
free and résuméd, I'm here now with black dress shoes and

a fine tailored suit. Don't you think I look like you? Here is my merit, here
is my college degree, here is my jail-time receipt. Am

I not what you were expecting? Am I too clean, too smart to end up with
marks on my record, to somehow choose the wrong

answer, to somehow not look the part? My crime is mine, a mistake where
I've already paid the price, where I took every

assumption made about me and put that person in solitude. I'm here
now—just me, hoping for an opportunity earned instead

of stolen, but will it be profitable to employ a felon like me, when my
body in a cell is worth more than my agency?

Dear Applicant

This is not a job offer.
I am sorry to inform you,
but we have moved on with another candidate.

I can't say if you are our #1 candidate,
but nepotism is still a thing in 2023
so like, thank you for being understanding.

Please know that we have hired the owner's son
who has already skimmed off the margins
and left our organization broken.

Think of this as a favor,
one where you don't have to blackmail
old grannies out of their little retirement.

Remember that we can't exploit you,
force infinite hours of unpaid overtime
with no breaks if you don't work for us.

Trust that this family business
specializes in back adjustments
à la very sharp knives.

We shall keep your application on file,
in the event, we have an opening again,
but we never look at it.

Good luck in all your future endeavors
and take this notice as the cessation
of all our communication.

Sincerely,
Every Hiring Manager About to Quit

A Memory of the Job Cycle

narrated by

Sir David Attenborough,
his soft voice twinkles in your ears:

*now watch, deep dive into regretful dreams, as the
days peak and lull, as you, oh, pitiful you, rewinds
your day*

ten:
congratulations! adulation,
joy a great geyser of cheer!
you're hired;
you're perfect;
you've been acquired!

nine:
you interview
nervous sweat crawls down your back;
peanut butter answers stick to the roof of your mouth;
questions in the same language as a duck's quack.

eight:
you apply
unease cuts like a rusty nail;
you forgot to get an updated tetanus shot;
you pray for once you don't fail.

seven:
you search
you're hopped up on coffee, box wine, and anxiety;
unqualified for jobs like a dull guillotine's blade;
in your fear, you wonder what's sobriety.

six:
you're unemployed
EDD almost spells dead;
takes too long to qualify;
you eat suspicious somewhat moldy bread instead.

Sir David Attenborough eulogizes your dreams:

> *if I could tell you the future, I would but history*
> *repeats itself just like you repeat yourself*
> *in your long string of demeaning jobs.*

five:
you're fired
you're not allowed back to your desk;
you're handed your things in a box;
ex-coworkers sigh, ex-bosses sneer grotesque.

four:
you're warned
any error will be your end;
you overthink and blink too much;
you miss the mark, the unbendable bends.

three:
you're overwhelmed
you've asked for guidance;
the company is short-staffed;
a co-worker suggests you be silent.

Sir David Attenborough heaves breath out of him in defeat:

> *you are not silent, you speak up,*
> *you ask question after question, oh, survival of the*
> *fittest*

two:
you train
they repurpose videos from the early 90s;
you're not sure when to use a pager;
the actors say it's only for crises.

one:
you start
your lipstick is a professional pink;
your dress a standard brown with gray tweed;
you're here to work and not think.

rewind
congratulations! adulation,
joy a great geyser of cheer!
you're hired;
you're perfect;
you've been acquired!

Sir David Attenborough speaks, his voice embracing your soul:

hold on to this moment, please always remember that you are someone strong, that you are somebody brave. that your time on earth proves to the universe that you are more than nothing. you are more than capitalism, more than greed, more than an expendable commodity. your value of worth not connected to productivity.

you are more than job hunting.

Acknowledgments

Thank you to my family for being by my side when I first tried to join the workforce in 2016.

Thank you to my partner for encouraging me to write this book and attend poetry events with me.

Thank you to Brenda Vaca and Riot of Roses Publishing for giving my book space.

Thank you to Community Literature Initiative for giving me the space to work on my poetry. Thank you to Camari Carter-Hawkins and Hiram Sims for being my teachers.

Thank you to James Coats for being my writing partner.

Thank you to Elle B. Parker for editing and organizing my poems into this narrative.

Thank you to Emily Anne Evans for interior design, cover design, and ePub formatting. Thank you to Jordan Roth for the cover design too.

Thank you to DJ Soulo for recording and editing the audiobook.

And finally, thank you readers for your support and time.

I hope to see you soon.

About the Author

Anastasia Helena Fenald (b. 1992) is a second-generation Ukrainian-Hispanic-American poet from California's windy High Desert. She has a B.A. in Global Studies from the University of Riverside, California (2014) and an M.A. in Globalization and Development from the University of Sheffield, United Kingdom (2015). Known for her energetic attitude and poignant poems, she spends most of her free time devouring fanfiction, performing at open mics, and forgetting to drink water until bedtime.

Her first poetry collection *Help Me, I'm Here: Poems to Myself*, was published by the World Stage Press. She has also been published in *Sheila-Na-Gig Online Journal*, *Acid Verse Literary Journal*, The Sims Library of Poetry's anthology *Poems in Praise of Libraries*, innateDIVINITY books' anthology *A Case for the Personhood of Trees*, *A Thousand Flowers Anthology*, Lit Stack, and more.

The Art of Job Hunting is her second poetry collection.

Go to her website www.lospoetry.com for updates about Anastasia Helena Fenald and discover new poets in her poetry directory.

Follower her on:
X/Twitter: @anastasiafenald
Instagram: @anastasiafenald
TikTok: @anastasia.fenald
Email: ana@lospoetry.com

About the Publisher

Riot of Roses Publishing House was founded in 2021 specifically to amplify the stories of historically silenced voices.

Xicana owned. Mujerista focused. For the people.

We publish books to heal and liberate others.

Read our rebellion.

RIOT OF ROSES
PUBLISHING HOUSE

SEJATNGA
UNCEDED TONGVA TERRITORY
SOUTH WHITTIER, CALIFORNIA

www.riotofrosespublishinghouse.com